BELLE'S IN THE

WIND

BY

BELLE CHERY

Copyright © 2018 by Belle Chery

All rights reserved. This book or any portion thereof may not be reproduced or used in any manner whatsoever without the express written permission of the author.

ISBN: 978-1-7336216-0-1

BELLE'S IN THE WIND

Authors Biography:

BELLE'S IN THE WIND by Belle Chery is the debut title of Haitian-born writer, Ms. Chery. This creation is an original collection of poems from adolescence; balancing loss, betrayal, life and LOVE as she struggles to adapt to a foreign Universe with an alien dialect, while finding her purpose. Although Chery earned her college degree at John Jay College of Criminal Justice, she has been using creative writing as an effective outlet since childhood. She hopes, Belle's in the Wind can help young adults find their inner voice through self expression as she did.

Table of Contents

Suffering Women	III
Come Home	IV
Why	VI
Trust	VIII
This Town	IX
Lie	XI
Poison	XIII
Haunted	XV
Not The One	XVI
Time to Time	XVII
Life	XIX
Growth	XXIII
A Friend	XXIV
Christmas	XXVI
New Year	XXVIII
You	XXIX
Think About You	XXX
Ideal	XXXI
Wish	XXXIII
Dreamer	XXXIV
Daily	XXXV
Prayer	XXXVI

Serenade everything you love with

liquid passion.

Life is a waterfront,

Sometimes there are waves,

Sometimes there is calm.

Suffering Women

Stealth, Stale Stench,

Broken Cement Walls

Blistered Burnt Flesh, Ends Prologue.

Come Home

Home seems so far away
Almost like a fairy tale,
One you can never go back to,
There was a time when home was
really home,
Organic markets flowing
freely on the broken pavements,
fresh smell of home made pate'
before the rooster roars it's morning blues
Playing marbles
while eating fresh, sweet, succulent mango's
from behind our two story house,
now life feels like hell
Place filled with enough stress to sell
Obligations artificial,
Pay off's low
I don't know where I heard this saying

But the grass is not always greener
If only I could go back in time
I'd be back home, doing just fine
But for you,
maybe it's not too late
And for that, I still have faith.

Why

I'm crying and I don't know why
It hurts but I don't deny
My chest feels acidic
Holding back these tears, is a losing battle
I want to know
Why is there so much pain?

I need to shout,

I need to scream,

I think I'm going insane

Like someone I trust unplugged my life support

The worst pain of all

is the fire burning on the inside

My synapses

The heart and mind won't abide

Heart Attack? The mirror gives a

different diagnosis

My heart is blasted in pieces

You did this to me,

I'm crying and I know why.

Trust

What is the meaning of this?
Was it something, I missed?
It seems as though, When God gave this out
I wasn't there to see
What was it all about?
People say;
Trust me. Believe me.
But what's trust?
Why is it so hard to regain?
And since nothing is promised,
why not stick to lust?
Why work to build it, bit by bit,
When a single blow can destroy it?
Is it how life trusts nature for protection?
Or when you trust me for affection?
Tell me again, what is trust?

This Town

There's a lot of anger in town

Doesn't seem to be anything,

anyone can do,

Anger turns smiles into wretched scowls

When uncontrollable things

become unbearable stings

What I can't seem to understand

How did anger get so high in demand?

It tears people apart,

it's supposed to pass in time,

Transforming into love

When anger shows it's distorted face,

Rid yourself of it

with quickened pace.

Lie

Why do you lie to me?

I thought I could count on you

I thought I could trust you,

I thought you would lead

Instead you played a dangerous game,

a dirty trick

My trust for you,

dwindled down to just a few,

memories

Almost forgetting how good it felt having it all

I used to think we'd stay together

Fooled into thinking things would get better

You lied so many times

The Truth, The Lies

Crisscrossed with every line

I want to break free

Your echoes won't let me be
I can't grip why you lie
My love for you is slowly beginning to die
fading
Maybe someday,
you'll find your truth
Or, you'll just run out of lies.

Poison

These feelings inside are
painfully burning me up
What was this, Some sick joke?
Everyone was in it but me
They said without it, there was no purpose
More valuable than money
Without it, you'll never be happy'
Of course it was too good to be true
I should've ran until my feet went numb
Find a dark hole and hide,
Curiosity got the best of me
Tempted for a taste of what is could be
Love, they called it
Passion, they called it
Tortured, is what all I felt
Lies and deceit

I wanted to taste love for myself,

I guzzled it down whole

Fire seeping through my veins

Wishing I stayed away

Love, no; venom, yes.

Now what?

Who has the antidote?

Haunted

I cry at the thought of losing you

though,

you're not even mine

for a sliver of time you were

I yearned to feel the tenderness of your kiss

and the sweetness of your love

Lucid dreams of waking up to you haunts me

Day after day, thoughts of you swirls round and round...

You've burned your mark on my heart

I've stopped trying to get you out my mind

Long ago, long ago

My family think it's a shame

Sometimes, I too,

feel the same

grim, gloomy, bottomless, haunting.

Not The One

Could you have guessed,

You'd be the one I'd fall for?

Should I have known,

You'd be my downfall?

So vulnerable

So fragile, So broken

you were

I was too blind to see,

really, truly, cruelly

You were only using me.

Time to Time

Time to time, you'll get by
Never feeling high
Time to time, you'll feel like you can fly
with never having to try
Time to time, you will see sometimes,
you just have to let things be
you won't always get the prize

Time to time,

you'll feel you won't have the
power to go on

But a little time, and you will heal

for then you'll understand
you must always use the word "can"
Time to time,
Time to time the world feels dreamy
Time to time we get too lull,

too at ease

we forget,

that when time runs out,

our time runs out.

Life

Life is a big challenge

obstacles, we learn to manage

When things go wrong

We think we're not strong,

When things go bad

We forget the good we've had,

Life is a difficult test

When things fall apart

You might want to give up

But life is a quest

The harder you fight, the tougher it gets

The goal is to be your best

Life wouldn't happen,

if you couldn't prevail

Life is a challenge

But in the end, you must sail

XXI

XXII

Growth

Learn to grow by not accepting disrespect

Learn by rejecting neglect

Stand for what's right

Stand with all your might

Learn how to let the past go

Cherish the present

Learn to grow by helping others even if they don't

Learn to care and uphold

learn to master

the roaring planes of love

Learn from the mistakes

stop putting happiness at stake

Learn to demand what you want

Growth is when you've realize,

everyday's a question

in this vale full of blessings.

A Friend

When is doubt

You always helped me find my route

If I wanted to whisk free

You'd always set me free

Together

we'd always blend

Because in you,

I had a friend

With you by my side;

I always tried. I never cried.

Because in you, I had a friend

When I said "a friend I didn't need"

You saw through the tales that seep

With you,

I shared my darkest thoughts

With you,

I shared my deepest secrets

The hurt you helped me leave behind

We go around in strife for reasons

You showed me how to open my heart

it hit me then, how good it's been

Because in you, I had a friend.

Christmas

What is the time of year
when everyone's excited?

The time of year you put your problems behind

The time of year when everyone's united

The time of year when peace and love

both combined

This time of year is December twenty fifth

A time that some say is a myth
A time other's believe are for gifts
The one day you put away all of your
tasks and business

A time to spend with family and friends

A time of love and laughter with no end

But if you are away from kin

you'll always have friends,

who cares,

and are there,

Just in time,

to celebrate your presence.

New Year

I've traveled vicariously

I've loved passionately

I've kissed sensually

I've laughed whole heartily

And I've abundantly made lasting

                                        memories.

You

When I see your face

I feel like I'm in a daze

When I hear your voice

It feels like an invisible force

so strong in its love

it leaves me with no clue

not knowing what I've gotten myself into

Then I hear your words

They remind me of singing blue birds

The prettiest song I've ever heard

makes me stop and pray

that I never lose you from this day

No matter what I do, I hope you'll stay

You're a remarkable one,

I'd be lost if you were gone.

Think About You

Thinking about you is unyielding
You've torn out my heart
You've snatched out my lungs
Yet, I still think about you
You've wounded my soul
You've made my thoughts so cold
inside feels so empty, hallow
As if I was no-one worth to know
Still, you've rented the space in my head
You've ripped my insides
bruised my outside

I'm afraid to know another's touch

Yet, I think about you
I think about you,
I think about you
I think about how, I think of you a rue.

xxx

Ideal

I've watched you from the corner of my orb

Most handsome suitor in the vault

Your visage, a majestic gift from reality

Your chest ample and husk

brown eyes, glisters while dancing in the sunlight

with every nod

a rare sensation

The richest silk for the finest man

The finest gems for the softest hands

Your skin as rich as a black pearl

The most swain of them all

To live in your world, if only for eternity

I've watched you out of the corner of my orb

Your smile will light up the darkest chamber

in human form

There's still no denying your divinity.

Wish

I made a wish for you today
I hope that it comes pure
A wish I yearned would bind with you,
a captivating lure
I didn't wish for fame or fortune
Although, it was a thought
A thought that came along with caution
but then I made a halt
I wished for you to have the World
The vast, the narrows, and all the twirls
I wished for you to live above,
gain wisdom, gain care,
but most of all, it was your flame
I wanted you to share.

Dreamer

I dreamt of you today

We had sun, we had shine

Warm glassy sand between our toes

Cool air against our cheeks

Eyes glossy, you turned to me

Loud waves crashing along the shore

though your lips were moving,

It was hard to hum a sound

As you stumbled on what you wanted to say

you whispered "I love you" like a summer breeze

The world once calm

My mind once racing,

freeze

I dreamt of this a million nights

today I was awake.

Daily

It's hard to get by, if you don't cry

When you cry, you're perceived as weak

You're taught to be strong, you're told to be tough

Everyday's a loop,

you get up and do it,

you go out and go through it

a constant need to prove this and that

Never expecting a kiss or pat

You go round and round with nothing else

the endless boundless cycle restarts

Daily.

Prayer

Dear God above,

The King of life and love

I'm saying this prayer to you

Because another day

I can't get through

Desperately,

you I need

My heart yearns for your lead

I wake up wishing for an end while I rest my head

I wonder If my angel you'll ever send

I pray for your blessings

and hope you accept me in the heavens

Dear God above

This note I've sent through a dove

as I spill my pain on this sheet

The days I'll count

till you'll make my life complete.

From great pain, CREATIVITY

DERIVES.

You Have To Keep Loving!

-The Universe.

ACKNOWLEDGMENTS

Thanks to my mom for always watching over me, even though she is nowhere near. P for keeping my books full of thoughts safe for years. Last but not least, me, for believing in my myself. Always believe in yourself, even if you are the only one who does. Know who you are and no one else can tell you different.

La Fin

www.ingramcontent.com/pod-product-compliance
Lightning Source LLC
LaVergne TN
LVHW041500070426
835507LV00009B/724